Potty Training Paradise With Jaela and Grandma

Rochelle Robinson

AuthorHouse™
1663 Liberty Drive
Bloomington, IN 47403
www.authorhouse.com
Phone: 1 (833) 262-8899

Because of the dynamic nature of the Internet, any web addresses or links contained in this book may have changed since publication and may no longer be valid. The views expressed in this work are solely those of the author and do not necessarily reflect the views of the publisher, and the publisher hereby disclaims any responsibility for them.

Any people depicted in stock imagery provided by Getty Images are models, and such images are being used for illustrative purposes only.
Certain stock imagery © Getty Images.

This book is printed on acid-free paper.

ISBN: 978-1-4389-0050-6 (sc)

Print information available on the last page.

Published by AuthorHouse 09/26/2020

authorHOUSE®

I dedicate this book to my precious granddaughter,

Jaela Janae Robinson.

She was my inspiration for writing this book.

DEDICATION

I dedicate this book to JAELA's parents:

My son, Jermaine

And

Larissa

Thank you both for blessing me

with my precious granddaughter

ABOUT THE AUTHOR

The author is a mother, wife, and grandmother. She is very family oriented. She loves to write. She has been writing poetry for over 20 years. She writes poems for holidays, birthdays, church programs, funerals, and just for fun.

She is very creative. She loves children and they love to be around her. Her nieces and nephews love to come and visit "Auntie Rocky". Whether it's a few days or a week this author will make it a fun-filled visit with her creative ideas. One summer her niece who lives out of town came to visit. Her parents couldn't get her to drink water. Creative Rochelle Robinson came up with a fun-filled family activity that had her niece begging for cups of water within 24 hours. The secrets will be revealed in her next children's book.

Potty Training Paradise
With Jaela and Grandma

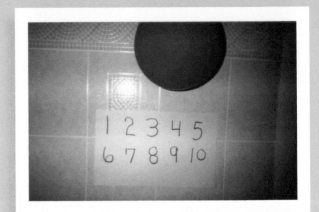

1 2 3 4 5
6 7 8 9 10

Potty Training Paradise

One (1), Two (2), Three (3),
It's potty training time for me.

Four (4), Five (5), Six (6),
I think I'm going to like this.

Seven (7), Eight (8), Nine (9),
I'm going to do just fine.

The last number is Ten (10),
I'm ready to begin.

Turn the bathroom into a fun room.

Decorate the walls and get some balloons.

Potty training can be fun.

If you know the way it should be done.

Make it like potty training paradise.

Your child will enjoy it and everything will be nice.

Some days the bathroom is our clubhouse.
We tip toe in quiet as a mouse.

Then we yell out "No Boys Allowed."
This is privacy time; we don't need a crowd.

We turn off the lights and pull out our flashlights.
We do shadow puppets on the wall...what a delight!

When she uses the potty, "I did it Grandma" is what she says,
Then we yell out "Hip! Hip! Hooray!"

Sometimes I make potty time reading time.
We read books and sing some rhymes.

One time she had to go to the potty and she had this puzzled look.
I said, "What's wrong?" She said, "I need my book!"

I tape posters and paper all around the bathroom walls.
While she sits on the potty she colors and draws.

We look at her drawings and we say, "Oooooo Weeee."
As she does her "do" on the potty.

Don't rush your lil' one and know that accidents will happen.
Sometimes at night the bed will get dampened.

Just make potty training fun,
Please don't pressure your daughter or your son.

Potty training takes time, you know.
Be patient as you train your child to go.

A-B-C-D-E-F-G

When I use the potty I sing my A-B-C's.

H-I-J-K-L-M-N-O-P

Singing makes potty training fun for me.

Q-R-S-T-U-V

Learning to use the potty can be lovely.

W-X-Y-Z

I'll be potty trained speedily.

Potty Training
Award
Presented
to
JAELA

Hip! Hip! Hooray!

I did a good job today.

Hip! Hip! Hooray!

I'm doing great on the potty training I must say.

Hip! Hip! Hooray!

Give me a reward, okay!

I love my Grandma and she loves me.
She always comes to the potty and waits with me.

She makes me laugh all the time.
She sits in there and reads me rhymes.

My Grandma makes potty training like paradise.
My Grandma is patient and very nice.

Grandma and I make potty time a time to pray.
We thank God for a beautiful day.

I say, "Thank you Jesus" and "Hallelujah", too.
My Grandma says this is something good to do.

My Grandma prays for me.
I pray for her and the rest of my family.

I thank Jesus that potty training is fun.
This is the end. Our book is done.

THE END

Printed in the United States
By Bookmasters